T0352577

ORO Editions
Publishers of Architecture, Art, and Design
Gordon Goff: Publisher

www.oroeditions.com
info@oroeditions.com

Published by ORO Editions

Authors: McLain Clutter, Cyrus Peñarroyo, Robert Fishman, and Clare Lyster
Book Design: McLain Clutter and Cyrus Peñarroyo
Project Coordinator: Alejandro Guzman-Avila
Managing Editor: Jake Anderson

10 9 8 7 6 5 4 3 2 1 First Edition

ISBN: 978-1-951541-65-1

Color Separations and Printing: ORO Group Ltd.
Printed in China.

ORO Editions makes a continuous effort to minimize the overall carbon footprint of its publications. As
part of this goal, ORO Editions, in association with Global ReLeaf, arranges to plant trees to replace those
used in the manufacturing of the paper produced for its books. Global ReLeaf is an international campaign
run by American Forests, one of the world's oldest nonprofit conservation organizations. Global ReLeaf is
American Forests' education and action program that helps individuals, organizations, agencies, and corporations improve the local and global environment by planting and caring for trees.

Shaped Places of Carroll County New Hampshire

McLain Clutter
Cyrus Peñarroyo

ORO EDITIONS

Shaped Places of Carroll County New Hampshire is a spatio-political satire that speculates on the complex reciprocity between who we are and where we live; between the identities of political subjects and the built environments that support them. The project draws upon a seemingly unlikely combination of protagonists and references–from Frank Stella to early 20th century urbanist Mikhail Aleksandrovich Okhitovich, and from American formalism to critical geography. In what follows, these disparate sources are placed into dialogue around common themes and pure coincidences. In doing so, latent connections between discrete discourses are identified, historical happenstance is exploited, and a-political aesthetic traditions are willfully distorted towards overt politico-geographic goals. The project narrative is structured in four distinct parts. Throughout each, common themes emerge and complexly intertwine, such as the dialogue between shape and content, urban and rural territories, and populations and the precincts in which they are counted. These themes inform the design of three linear cities in Carroll County, within the swing state of New Hampshire.* In each linear city, population is geometrically organized at a geographic scale to carefully prescribed ends. Shape and content forge a complex reciprocity.

* Carroll County was established in 1840, and named after Charles Carroll of Carrollton. Carroll, who lived from 1737 to 1832, was one of the Founding Fathers of the United States, a signer of the Declaration of Independence, and a wealthy Maryland landowner whose fortune benefited significantly from the extraction of labor from enslaved Africans. At the time of contact with white Europeans, the land that now constitutes Carroll County was occupied by the native Abenaki people.

Town of
WINDHAM

MUNICIPAL CENTER

CHECK OUT
OUR
SCARECROWS

Visionary Shaped Places in New England
from the Puritans to Clutter & Peñarroyo

Robert Fishman

Anyone looking to the Shaped Places of Carroll County for an updated version of a New England village with tasteful allusions to white clapboard and green shutters will be surprised—if not shocked—by this radical "provocation" as designers McLain Clutter and Cyrus Peñarroyo rightly term it. For these Places have been Shaped by a unique synthesis of the linear city theories of the Soviet "deurbanists" of the 1920s and 1930s with the formal logic of Frank Stella's Irregular Polygon paintings of the 1960s. Around this synthesis the two designers have envisaged diverse contemporary building types that would bring together diverse elements of American society from blue-collar outdoors types to upper-middle-class sophisticates—all organized through repeating linear city planning modules. The result is an ironic utopia—an urban/rural collage designed to overcome the deep political divisions in the United States which separate town and country.

If the form of the Shaped Places represents a radical departure from anything resembling the historic New England village, I would argue that there is another sense in which the radical urbanism of Shaped Places revives certain themes whose Puritan pedigree goes back to the sect's 17th century "errand into the wilderness." Long before Karl Marx or the Soviet deurbanists, the Puritans had aimed at using shape and content to overcome the division between town and country. They were preoccupied with joining together the diverse elements of their premodern society into a single godly community which—at least in their original conceptions—was carefully shaped around the form of a quasi-medieval "village" incorporating farmers, craftsmen, and merchants centering on an austere "Meeting House" (both church and community center), all surrounded by tilled fields and forests.

This tightly centered form evolved in the 18th and 19th centuries into the more expansive and typical unit of New England local governance: the "Town" or township which included within its thirty or more square miles a range of hamlets, villages, and other well-defined settlements as well as extensive farmland and woodlands. As Lewis Mumford observes in *The City in History*, the New England Town "brought into existence, and in many places kept going for two centuries, a balance between rural and urban occupations, as well as an internal balance of population and usable land."[1] For Mumford and his colleagues in the influential Regional Planning Association of America (RPAA) of the 1920s and 1930s, the New England Town was not only an object for historical analysis and praise, but a starting-point for their critique of the industrial metropolis and a template for the decentralized society they wished to build. Like their contemporaries the Soviet deurbanists, the RPAA arrived at a highway-based "linear city" post-urban form as their preferred design to overcome the division between city and countryside.

It's important to recognize that the New England Town that Mumford praises was the product of a long evolution where the traditional English village was transformed in the New World not only by Puritan ideals of a godly community but also by the more materialistic opportunities that the abundance of land seized violently from the Native Americans provided. As a unit of local government, the typical New England Town began with a land grant, i.e., a purchase by a group of potential settlers of a large tract of wilderness, usually at least 30 square miles, which they bought directly from the King of England or (more commonly) from the King's agents in New England. The settlers began by identifying an initial site within this large area, almost always on a river that could provide both transportation and water-power where they constructed first a Meeting House for both worship and secular purposes. Around the Meeting House would be clustered the homes of the settlers, with extensive gardens. Further off would be the "great lots," the main farm plots for each farming household, who would also possess a more remote "woodlot" on the forested slopes.[2]

But this initial pattern quickly broke down as the settlers sought to enlarge their "great lots" to better accommodate their growing and very profitable cattle herds. The farm families moved their homes from the early village to their expanded "great lots," creating the now-familiar pattern of isolated farmhouses in the midst of their fields. This left the original villages "very thin," as one Puritan minister complained, with only the Meeting House and perhaps a gristmill and sawmill and a few houses left. Nevertheless, the Meeting House and its mandatory Sunday service remained the heart of the community, and when all the land within a wagon-ride of the Meeting House had been taken up, a group of younger sons and other settlers hived off to form a separate nucleus at a suitable site somewhere else within the extensive unsettled lands of the township. The separate villages with their farming outliers came together once a year for the famous New England Town Meetings which exemplified direct democracy in the New World.[3]

As prosperity increased in the 18th and early 19th centuries, the "very thin" original villages attracted a new set of storekeepers, lawyers and doctors, school teachers, blacksmiths, carpenters and others serving a now-thriving rural population. At this point the "New England village" as commonly conceived was built. The squat Meeting House was replaced with the white clapboard Congregational Church whose impressive steeple rose over a village green surrounded by the substantial whitewashed and green-shuttered homes and businesses of the village middle class. Nevertheless, these "centers" like Conway Center rarely grew beyond 2,000 people, leaving the larger Town of Conway and similar New England Towns with the characteristic balance that Mumford praises of village centers located at key transportation crossroads (rivers or turnpike roads) in the midst of farmland and woodland.[4]

By the mid-18th century when Carroll County, New Hampshire was settled, the Puritan fervor had faded, and the prospect of material gain had increased. As an early historian of Carroll County put it, the older coastal towns of New Hampshire,

> ...after they had been settled a hundred years seemed to the active young men of 1760 to be thickly peopled. The best of the pine and oak had been cut down. With succeeding generations and increasing numbers the farms [in the older communities] had been divided and subdivided

1. Lewis Mumford, *The City in History* (New York: Harcourt, 1961), 332.
2. Charles Francis Adams et al., *The Genesis of the Massachusetts Town: And the Development of Town-Meeting Government* (J. Wilson and Son, 1892).
3. John W. Reps, *The Making of Urban America: A History of City Planning in the United States* (Princeton: Princeton University Press, 1965), chap. 5.
4. Georgia Drew Merrill, *History of Carroll County, New Hampshire* (Boston: W.A. Ferguson & Co., 1889).
5. Merrill, 469.

Conway, New Hampshire, 1896
From a panoramic map in the Norman Leventhal Map Center, Boston Public Library

until the young and enterprising turned their thoughts to [Carroll County]...[5]

By the time of the American Revolution Carroll County had been divided into large Townships and settled in the characteristic decentralized New England way. Of Frank Stella's three shaped canvases referenced by Clutter and Peñarroyo, "Conway" designates both the Town of Conway (71.7 square miles) and Conway Center, a village (3.1 square miles), now also termed a "census designated place." Sanbornville (1.6 square miles) and Union (0.32 square miles) are both villages/census designated places within the Town of Wakefield (44.7 square miles).[6]

A magnificent panoramic map of Conway Center and its environs from 1890 now in the Norman Leventhal Map Center of the Boston Public Library shows why Mumford and his RPAA colleagues regarded the New England Town as a better model for 20th century growth than either the factory town or the industrial metropolis whose explosive growth during 19th century had dominated American urbanism. As one sees in the panoramic view, Conway Center in 1890 was a farm-to-market hub but also a site for small-scale manufacturing that utilized water-power from its two rivers to process timber brought down from the hillsides. Yet the village maintained an architectural unity based on a fabric of two and three-story frame houses; a walkable scale; efficient railway connections to the rest of New England; and easy access to farmland and open space in one of the most beautiful landscapes in North America.

The 20th century visionary regional planning that turned places like Carroll County into prototypes for a new kind of American linear city was not the work of Mumford himself but of his colleague in the RPAA, Benton MacKaye.[7] Now mostly remembered for his design and advocacy of the Appalachian Trail, MacKaye (1879-1975) lived almost his whole life in Shirley Center, the main settlement in the still-preserved New England Town of Shirley, Massachusetts. Although MacKaye firmly supported the regionalist aim of moving population out of the crowded city into the countryside, he was alarmed by the 1920s-style sprawl of "ribbon development" on the highways out of Boston that threatened to turn the countryside into what we now call sprawl.

His remedy was "the Townless Highway," one of the inspirations for our system of interstates—though devised for a wholly different purpose.[8] The Townless Highway would not only bypass existing village centers, but it would be limited-access to prevent ribbon development along it. The carefully spaced on-and-off ramps would feed directly into newly built planned "New Towns," the RPAA's 1920s version of Ebenezer Howard's Garden City. A prototype New Town was already under construction: Radburn, New Jersey (1928), designed by Henry Wright and Clarence Stein.[9]

As in Howard's original Garden City concept from the 1890s, the New Town would be a "marriage of town and country" in Howard's phrase, a relatively dense and walkable place surrounded by a perpetual greenbelt to preserve the access to farmland and other open space beyond. The overcrowded central cities like Boston would "decant" into the New Towns, which would be linked for efficient industrial production by the Townless Highway, but whose regional planning would ensure a modern version of a landscape balanced between rural and urban that Mumford had praised in the New England Town.

It is surely no coincidence that the Soviet deurbanists and the American RPAA arrived at such similar linear city plans during the 1920s and 1930s. Both were seeking an alternative to the smoke-filled overcrowded industrial metropolis; both were deeply influenced by the Garden City movement and such related figures as the Russian anarchist Peter Kropotkin, author of *Fields, Factories and Workshops* (1899); and both understood that technology permitted a radical decentralization of production and distribution along linear lines of transportation and communication, an insight that Le Corbusier would later develop in his linear cities of the 1940s. Thanks to America's rapid shift to automobiles and trucks, the RPAA as early as the 1920s could make the superhighway rather than the railroad its main linear organizing principle.

6. "New Hampshire 2010 Census," accessed November 2, 2020, https://www.census.gov/prod/cen2010/cph-2-31.pdf. Table 8.
7. Larry Anderson, *Benton MacKaye: Conservationist, Planner, and Creator of the Appalachian Trail*, Creating the North American Landscape (Baltimore: Johns Hopkins University Press, 2002).
8. Benton MacKaye, "The Townless Highway," *The New Republic* 62, no. 797 (March 12, 1930): 93–94.
9. Clarence S. Stein, *Toward New Towns for America*, [Rev. ed.] (New York: Reinhold Pub. Corp, 1957).

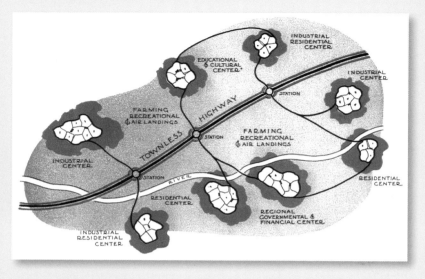

RPAA Linear City. Clarence Stein's 1942 re-drawing of Benton MacKaye's concept of the Townless Highway. Here, functionally specialized "centers" set in greenbelts connect to the linear highway hub.
Source: *Pencil Points* (1942).

American Linear City Modernism. Still from "The City" (1939) showing Greenbelt, MD.

The best insight into the MacKaye-RPAA vision is surely the famous documentary "The City," directed by Ralph Steiner and Willard Van Dyke with commentary by Mumford, commissioned by the American Institute of Planners (now the American Planning Association) and shown at the Science and Education Building of the 1939 New York World's Fair.[10] The film begins in MacKaye's own Shirley, Massachusetts, whose well-preserved center does a remarkably good job as a stage-set representing the premodern New England village with its close connection of town and country. The film then moves to depict the squalor and pollution of the factory town (steel mills outside Pittsburgh) and the inhuman crowding and stress of the industrial metropolis (New York City). But the film concludes with a return—not literally to Shirley Center—but to an ideal New Town (spliced together from Radburn and Greenbelt, Maryland, one of the New Deal "Greenbelt Towns").

The film's RPAA New Town glows with a modernist vernacular whose design principles draw on Catherine Bauer's hopeful synthesis in *Modern Housing* (1934). Thanks to linear city planning, there is no need for either metropolitan crowding or pollution or for suburban single-family sprawl. In this modest utopia, clean white functionalist garden apartments stand in ample landscaped lawns; there is also a generous public realm: schools, libraries, parks, community centers, cooperative stores and laundries. A (non-polluting) factory district stands in its own park, within walking distance of the homes. The communitarian and ecological virtues of the New England Town are recreated along the linear city with modern technology and planning.

What virtues do Clutter & Peñarroyo's Shaped Places celebrate? As I've suggested in this essay, one might look beyond the radically new design to see a deep commonality not only with the RPAA linear city but even with the New England Town. For all three, "shape and content form a complex reciprocity," as Clutter & Peñarroyo put it, based on a "marriage of town and country" that would bring together the urban and rural elements in their societies. In at least one respect, the Shaped Places are closer to the Puritan ideal than the RPAA Greenbelt Town. The progressive New Deal vision always emphasized a fundamental unity of "The People" and the Greenbelt Town appears in "The City" to be a classless society, with working class and middle-class families inhabiting the same modernist dwellings and sharing equally in the communal life of the Town.

For all their religious dissent, the Puritans were part of a hierarchical premodern society that was intensely aware of the different gradations of status and wealth, gradations that disappeared only in the Meeting House on Sundays where only one's personal relation with God counted. Like the Puritans, Clutter & Peñarroyo are intensely focused on social differences which are defined ironically in the language of consumer research, e.g. "childless middle-age couples with lucrative blue-collar jobs and modestly-priced houses." Far from hiding such differences under a uniform pattern of "modern housing" as in the Greenbelt Towns, they imagine radically different housing types to suit each category, from McMansions in *Sanbornville* for the well-paid blue-collar couple to the high-rise mixed use luxury condos of *Conway* for "multicultural upper-middle-class well-traveled couples."

Lacking a Puritan Meeting House and the hope of heaven to bring the diverse elements together, Clutter and Peñarroyo pin their hopes for unity on a dense, complex mashup of the different lifestyles and housing types. Thus, the blue-collar McMansions of *Sanbornville* adjoin a high-rise social housing block for multi-ethnic families with modest incomes; the glossy towers of *Conway* for the upper-middle-class adjoin other high-rises for back-to-nature agrarians, and hydroponic agriculture towers for growing lettuce, spinach, and cabbage. All these juxtapositions are contained within the limits of a linear city that juxtaposes city and countryside. In design and aspiration this is not the New England Town or the Greenbelt Town, but the Shaped Places lie recognizably within the territory first opened up by the Puritan John Winthrop and his 1630 vision of a transformed "city upon a hill."

2016 Presidential Election Results

Shaped Places of Carroll County New Hampshire

McLain Clutter & Cyrus Peñarroyo

New Hampshire

If you follow electoral politics, New Hampshire's geographic shape might be retinally burned into your consciousness. The notorious swing state remained purple on the U.S. presidential election map until late into the night on November 8, 2016. The state was finally awarded to Hillary Clinton by a margin of fewer than three thousand votes—less than one half of one percent of the voter turnout. This episode met two decades of indefinite political leanings in a state that was once considered staunchly Republican. In modern presidential elections, New Hampshire was awarded to Republican presidential candidates in all but three elections prior to 1992. In that year, presidential candidate Bill Clinton swung the state to the Democrat's side. This first Clinton candidacy initiated a pattern of uncertain political leanings that has persisted to this day. State and local elections are increasingly tight, and offices regularly flip between Republican and Democratic control in each election cycle.[1]

Several factors underlie New Hampshire's recently mercurial politics. The state is a battleground between an urban population of liberal persuasion and a fervently conservative-cum-libertarian contingency from rural areas. New Hampshire is also among

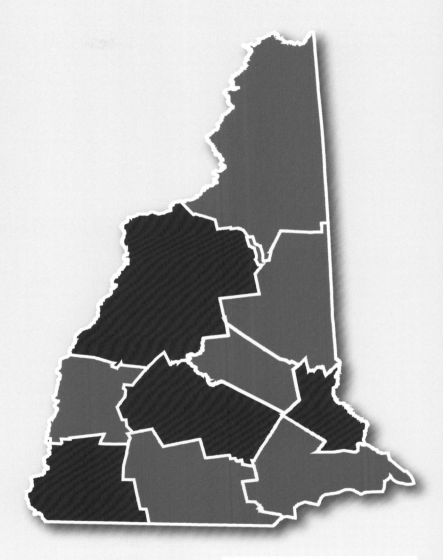

New Hampshire 2016 Presidential Election Results

the most white, least diverse states in the union. This fact alone should prompt critical reflection as to why a state so demographically divergent from the nation as a whole votes first in the Presidential primaries, thus holding disproportionate influence on the choice of an eventual nominee. But, like many states in the union, New Hampshire's population of people of color has grown precipitously over the past decade, largely concentrated in urban areas like Manchester and Nashua.[2] These non-white residents tend to vote along progressive and liberal lines. Such a divided body politic between rural and urban geographies is not unique. In this respect, the Granite State is a microcosm of the political geography of the United States as a whole. Journalists and political scientists alike have noted that the often-repeated narrative of a country split between the liberal coastal elite and more conservative populations in the country's "heartland" no longer stands. Instead, the political geography of the United States is sharply divided between cities and the countryside, especially as those distinctions align with differences in race and socioeconomic status.[3] In 2016, a similar percentage of voters cast their ballots for Hillary Clinton in congressional districts in downtown Wichita as in some districts in Manhattan.[4] Conversely, some districts in rural New Jersey voted as dark red as the Deep South. The country's divided political patterns are isomorphic to its divided patterns of urbanization.

1. Dan Barrick, Rebecca Lavoie, Natasha Haverty, "As New Hampshire Shifts to a Swing State, Why Do Legislative Lines Still Favor Republicans?" *New Hampshire Public Radio*. April 20, 2016. Accessed July 20, 2019. https://www.nhpr.org/post/new-hampshire-shifts-swing-state-why-do-legislative-lines-still-favor-republicans#stream/0
2. David Brooks, "Census Bureau estimates that 10% of New Hampshire is now a racial or ethnic minority." Concord Monitor. June 22, 2019. Accessed July 25, 2019. https://www.concord-monitor.com/mintority-nh-demographics-census-26432120
3. Josh Kron, "Red State, Blue City: How the Urban-Rural Divide Is Splitting America." *The Atlantic*, November 30, 2012. Accessed November 12, 2019. https://www.theatlantic.com/politics/archive/2012/11/red-state-blue-city-how-the-urban-rural-divide-is-splitting-america/265686/

Justin Davidson. "Cities Vs. Trump, Red state, blue state? The urban-rural divide is more significant." *New York Magazine Intelligencer*. Accessed November 12, 2019. https://nymag.com/intelligencer/2017/04/the-urban-rural-divide-matters-more-than-red-vs-blue-state.html Emily Badger, "How the Rural-Urban Divide Became America's Political Fault Line." *The New York Times*, May 21, 2019. Accessed, November 12, 2019. https://www.nytimes.com/2019/05/21/upshot/america-political-divide-urban-rural.html
4. Matthew Bloch, Larry Buchanan, Josh Katz, and Kevin Quealy, "An Extremely Detailed Map of the 2016 Election." *The New York Times*, July 25, 2018. Accessed July 1, 2019. https://www.nytimes.com/interactive/2018/upshot/election-2016-voting-precinct-maps.html#7.85/40.00/-74.77

1982

1992

2002

2004

2012

New Hampshire Senate Districts

In New Hampshire, as in many other states, the division between the rural and urban has been exacerbated by gerrymandering, a politico-geographic maneuver that seeks to ensure electoral power through the strategic design of voting districts, often purposely dividing population along starkly apparent lines of race and class.[5] Gerrymandering was originally named after the Massachusetts Governor Elbridge Gerry, who in 1812 signed a bill meant to create a district near Boston whose shape would assure victory to his own Democratic-Republican Party. Since this time, gerrymandering has been deployed to consolidate power or divide and diffuse opposition through the design of electoral districts across the nation, including in New Hampshire. A recent study showed that between the 2000 and 2016 elections, more and more congressional districts in New Hampshire have drifted toward increasingly extreme political positions, just as those districts have been redrawn to capture voters of similar political ideology.[6] Such actions make electoral politics all the more contentious and profoundly impact the political reality of the state through figuring geographic shapes to assure electoral victory to the reigning party. Shape and content forge a complex reciprocity.

Irregular Polygons

In 1963, the abstract artist Frank Stella spent a year in New Hampshire as visiting faculty at Dartmouth College. Shortly after this brief appointment, between 1965 and 1966, Stella produced a collection of paintings he named the Irregular Polygons. No doubt inspired by his time in the state, each painting within the series was named after a village in New Hampshire—Wolfeboro, Chocorua, Conway, Effingham, Moultonborough, Moultonville, Ossipee, Sandbornville, Sunapee, Tuftonboro, and Union. Each of the compositions was painted in four color variations, and every painting in the series is a three-dimensionally shaped canvas containing geometric bands of color within. The dynamic sculptural quality of the paintings and their chromatic heterogeneity marked a sharp departure from Stella's earlier work, often featuring black stripes on more statically composed shaped canvases.[7]

The Irregular Polygons are among Stella's most renowned paintings. And while this fame is no doubt due partially to innovations in color, composition, and shape, the Irregular Polygons are also well known for their reception by the art critic Michael Fried. Fried's criticism has been influential as it has been controversial, upholding a narrow conception of modernism that has been repeatedly criticized as exclusionary of all but the most elitist identities and subject positions. Nevertheless, the critic's thought profoundly impacted the American art world in the latter half of the twentieth century, and his work continues to be widely read today. To fully apprehend Fried's writing about Stella's canvases, it is first necessary to understand the intellectual lineage of Fried's work.

Michael Fried's art criticism was built upon a paradigm of formal autonomy in modern art with a well-developed discourse that was deeply indebted to the critic Clement Greenberg. According to Greenberg, who himself built upon the philosophy of Immanuel Kant, the central characteristic of modernity was self-criticality. Following this thesis, Greenberg asserted that modern art was properly understood as a self-critique or interrogation of the essential characteristics of each artistic medium. Writing in a twentieth century context in which painting's capacities of representational similitude had been overtaken by filmic media, Greenberg understood the enduring essential quality of painting to be flatness or surface. Thus, in order for a painting to be modern, it had to embrace an interrogation of its own surficial qualities. For example, in Greenberg's formulation a painting like Pablo Picasso's *The Accordionist* (1911) might be defined as properly modern because

5. Kim Soffen, "How racial gerrymandering deprives black people of political power." *The Washington Post*, June 9, 2016. Accessed July 25, 2019. https://www.washingtonpost.com/news/wonk/wp/2016/06/09/how-a-widespread-practice-to-politically-empower-african-americans-might-actually-harm-them/
6. Dan Barrick, Rebecca Lavoie, Natasha Haverty, "As New Hampshire Shifts to a Swing State, Why Do Legislative Lines Still Favor Republicans?" *New Hampshire Public Radio*. April 20, 2016. Accessed July 20, 2019. https://www.nhpr.org/post/new-hampshire-shifts-swing-state-why-do-legislative-lines-still-favor-republicans#stream/0
7. https://hoodmuseum.dartmouth.edu/news/2010/09/frank-stella-irregular-polygons
8. Clement Greenberg, "Towards a Newer Laocoon," in *The Collected Essays and Criticism*, Volume I: Perceptions and Judgments, 19391944, ed. John O'Brian (Chicago, IL: University of Chicago Press, 1986), 35.
9. Clement Greenberg, "Modernist Painting," in Frascina and Harrison, eds., *Modern Art and Modernism: A Critical Anthology* (New York: Harper and Row for the Open University, 1984), 5-10.

it affords changing impressions of pictorial depth and flatness, constantly agitating the canvas surface with flirtations of illusionist space that were elsewhere negated by the compositional logic of the painting.[8] For Greenberg, such formal maneuvers prohibited all meaning external to the form, making the *subject* of the painting its very surface. By resisting external meaning, Greenberg held that a painting could exist outside of the entanglements of base society, thus securing the status of high art.[9]

While working in the tradition of Greenberg, Fried met an art world significantly changed since the first half of the twentieth century. In his most famous essay, "Art and Objecthood" from 1966, Fried condemned the work of a group of emergent minimalist artists including Robert Morris and Donald Judd for the uncritical object-qualities of their sculpture, or the way their sculptures plainly embraced their own *objecthood*. Calling these artists "literalists," Fried deemed their sculptures problematic because of their uncritical assertions of *shape*. If Fried understood *form* as a rarified aesthetic quality that emerged in modern art through self-critique, *shape* was little more than a "fundamental property of objects."[10] Furthermore, by plainly and uncritically asserting shape, the literalist sculptures became merely prosaic objects amongst viewing subjects. This created a "theatrical" subject-object relationship that threatened the disciplinary autonomy of modern art by engaging the viewer, thus placing meaning exterior to the form, in the space and uncertainty of individual subjective experience.[11] Such an embrace of the diversity and contingency in meaning that would attend multiple subject positions was deeply problematic for Fried, a critic whose narrow conception of modernism was fundamentally exclusionary.[12]

10. Michael Fried, "Art and Objecthood,' *Artforum*, June 1967, pp. 14-15.
11. Ibid.
12. Criticism of the exclusionary nature of Fried's work has been broad, from Rosalind Krauss's reframing of the Greenbergian tradition in support of the minimalists Fried condemned, to Christa Noel Roberts's more recent interrogations of a latent homophobic sentiment within Fried's writing.
Rosalind Krauss, "Sense and Sensibility: Re-flections on Post '60's Sculpture," *Artforum*, November 1973, pp. 149-155.
Christa Noel Robbins,"The Sensibility of Michael Fried," *Criticism*, Volume 60, Number 4, Fall 2018, pp. 429-454.
13. Michael Fried, "Shape as Form," *Artforum*, November 1966, pp. 18-27.
14. Ibid.
15. Ibid, 22.
16. Ibid.

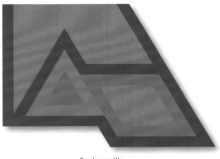

Sanbornville
Frank Stella
1966

Union
Frank Stella
1966

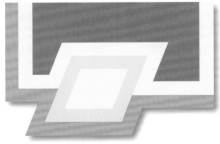

Conway
Frank Stella
1966

Offset

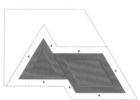

Offset

Continuity of color

Continuity of color

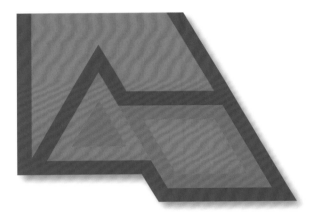

Sanbornville
Frank Stella
1966

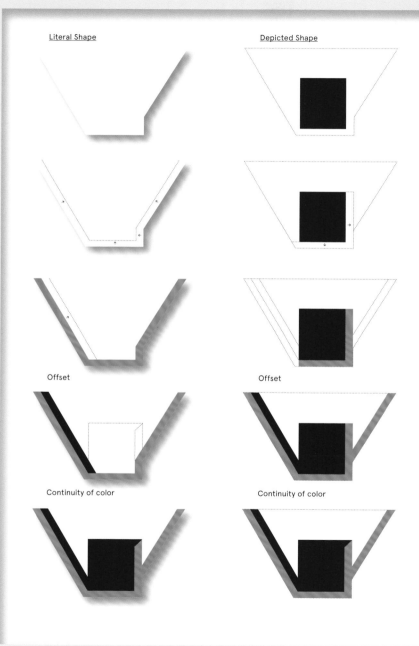

Literal Shape

Depicted Shape

Offset

Offset

Continuity of color

Continuity of color

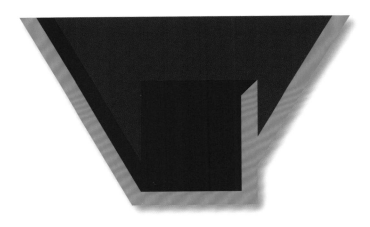

Union
Frank Stella
1966

Literal Shape

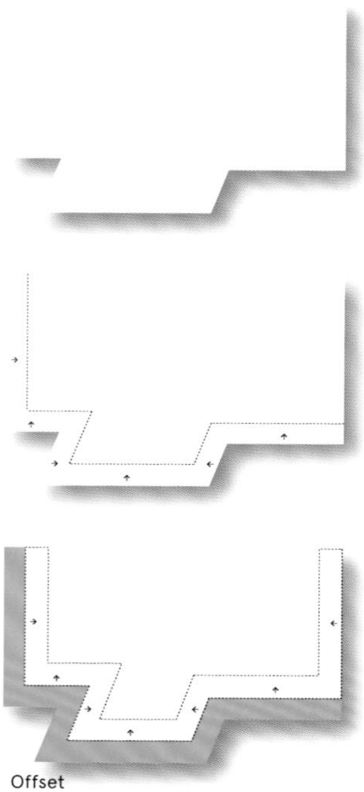

Depicted Shape

Offset

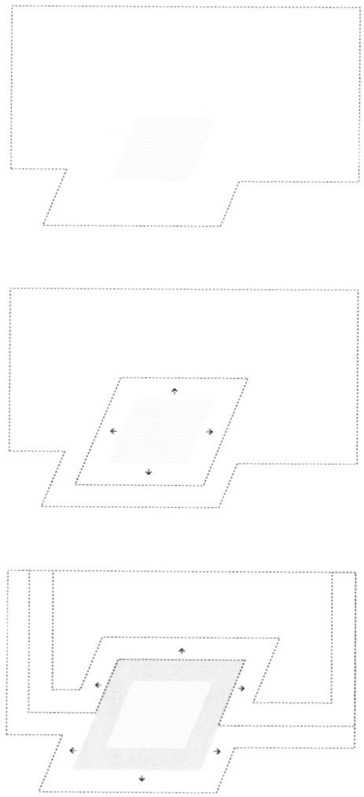

Offset

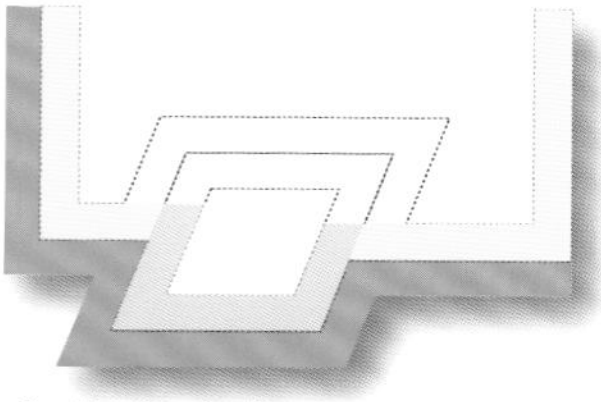

Continuity of color

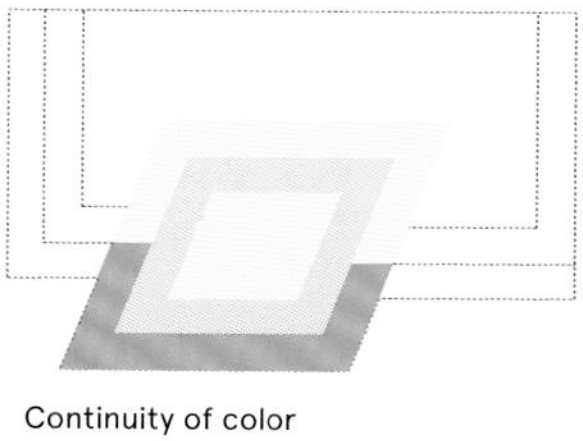

Continuity of color

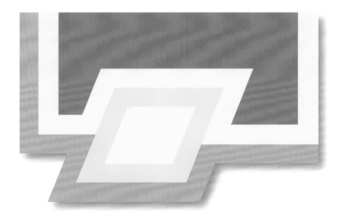

Conway
Frank Stella
1966

Shape soon became Fried's tortured preoccupation. He argued that the uncritical assertion of shape by the literalists necessitated a shift in the art-world, requiring modern art to embrace an interrogation of shape in order to reclaim its autonomy. Thus, for Fried, *shape* assumed a role in painting akin to *surface* in Clement Greenberg's art criticism. In an essay written immediately prior to "Art and Objecthood," "Shape as Form: Frank Stella's Irregular Polygons," Fried argued that Stella's Irregular Polygons were at the avant-garde of such self-critique of shape.[13] The critic described Stella's canvases through a dialectic between *depicted shape*, by which he meant the internal geometric stripe pattern of the painting, and *literal shape*, by which he meant the shape of the canvas itself, or what Fried termed "the shape of support." This latter category of shape, the shape of support, aligned with the inherent object-quality of all things that Fried found so uncritically embraced by the literalists.[14] Fried noted that in each Irregular Polygon painting it was impossible to determine whether the geometry of the stripes dictated the shape of the support or vise-versa. He wrote:

> "There are shapes that lie entirely inside the picture limits…just as there are others that partly coincide with the edge of the support. But neither kind of shape enjoys precedence over the other…both types of shape succeed or fail on exactly the same grounds—grounds that do not concern the relation of a given shape of the support seen in its entirety. Each, one might say, is implicated in the other's failure and strengthened by the other's success…"[15]

Fried later went on:

> "This is not to say that the shape of the support is either ignored or denied…but the way in which this is accomplished does not affirm the dependence of depicted or literal shape so much as it establishes an unprecedented continuity between them."[16]

Clutter & Peñarroyo

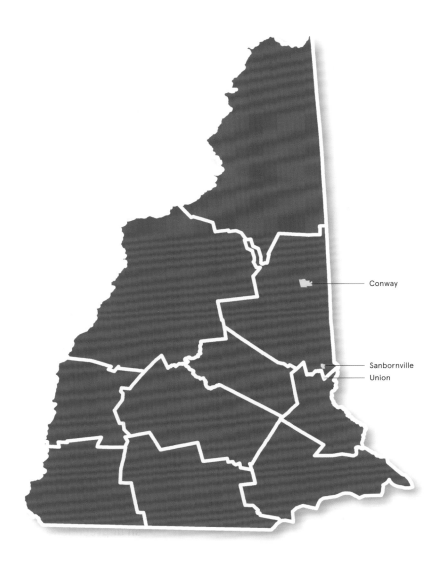

Conway

Sanbornville

Union

New Hampshire Congressional Districts

Fried's infatuation with this "unprecedented continuity" might seem pedantic. What could be gained through such a dialogue between "literal" and "depicted" shape? The answer lies in Fried's debt to his intellectual forebear, Clement Greenberg, as Fried was building directly on Greenberg's understanding of self-critique as the fundamental obligation of modern art. Through paintings in which it is impossible to determine whether the shape of the canvas dictated the content within, or vise-versa, Fried argued that Stella initiated a self-critique of shape in his paintings. For Fried, such a turn inward prohibited all meaning external to the form, exempting the work from everyday culture and society, and securing the status of high art. Shape and content forge a complex reciprocity.

Census Designated Places

It is highly unlikely that Michael Fried imagined that his writing about Frank Stella's work could be co-opted and brought to bear on issues of political geography. Indeed, Fried's entire discourse overtly resisted such entanglements. And yet, by championing the Irregular Polygons, Fried inadvertently opened a portal to the politico-geographic. Thus, what follows should be read as a willful distortion of Fried's intentions. Here, an art world discourse bent on exclusion and autonomy is applied to renegotiate who and what is allowed to be on the inside and outside of political territories.

As noted above, each painting within Stella's Irregular Polygons was named after a village in New Hampshire. All in Carroll County, three of these villages—Sandbornville, Union, and Conway—share their names with surrounding geographies called Census Designated Places (CDPs). CDPs are geographic units of demographic data collection created for use by the decennial U.S. Census. Thus, CDPs are one geography through which the federal government organizes population data under often politically charged demographic headings such as race, sex, age, and marital status. Unlike legally incorporated entities like cities, towns, or villages, a CDP does not have an elected government, nor legal status. They commonly contain at least one unincorporated town (a nominal town without legal status), and usually encompass both rural and relatively urban territories. Additionally, the borders of a CDP can be seemingly arbitrary. Unlike other geographic units of census data aggregation like Census Blocks or Census Tracts, CDPs might not be defined by sensible markers or physical features such as rivers or roads. And while the guidelines for establishing a CDP prescribe that they should not be *merely* administrative units, those that live within often do not self-identify as residing in a place with the CDPs name.[17] CDPs are relatively rare, and are used for census data aggregation only when other geographic units do not apply. They are wholly invented geographic entities created solely for the management of census demographic data about the population within.

Census data is used to guide a range of commercial and governmental applications. In doing so, all of the sometimes-contentious identity distinctions embedded in the data about race, sex, and more are instrumentalized. State and local governments might use census data to make decisions about infrastructure spending, the distribution of social services, the formulation of future disaster recovery plans, and more. Census data is used by the federal government to determine funding levels for farm and housing subsidies, education, veteran support, community economic development, and many other programs.[18] And at all levels of government, census data is used in the establishment of voting districts—where it is encountered by those that craft the gerrymandering practices discussed above.[19] Census data is also used by corporate entities

17. Federal Register. "Census Designated Place (CDP) Program for the 2010 Census-Final Criteria," February 2, 2008. Accessed August 10, 2019. https://www.federalregister.gov/documents/2008/02/13/E8-2667/census-designated-place-cdp-program-for-the-2010-census-final-criteria

18. Clinton Whitehouse Council of Economic Advisors. "The Uses of Census Data: An Analytical Review." April 1, 2000. Accessed August 11, 2019. https://clintonwhitehouse4.archives.gov/WH/EOP/CEA/html/censusreview.html

19. "Redistricting and Use of Census Data." National Conference of State Legislatures, Accessed August 11, 2019. https://www.ncsl.org/research/redistricting/redistricting-and-use-of-census-data.aspx

20. Hugh D. Hudson, *Blueprints and Blood: The Stalinization of Soviet architecture, 1917-1937*

(Princeton, NJ: Princeton University Press, 1994), 62.

21. Anatole Kopp has explained that the OSA discourse around urbanization at this time consisted of two opposing schools of thought, the urbanists and deurbanists. The former, guided by the theorist Leonid Sabsovich, advocated new cities consisting of vast communal housing blocks constructed around factories. This pattern of development would, theoretically, spread across the entire nation to eradicate the division between the rural and urban. The latter school of thought, the deurbanists, encompassed the majority of OSA. Championed by theorist Mikhail Aleksandrovich Okhitovich, the highly ideological ambitions of the deurbanists are of interest here. Anatolo Kopp, *Town and Revolution: Soviet Architecture and City Planning, 1917-1935* (New York: George Braziller. 1970), 168-178.

like ACXIOM, Claritas, and ESRI. These companies combine census data with consumer spending information and other data points to create statistical assemblages called market segmentation sets—commercial data sets describing bespoke consumer identities that are used for purposes ranging from the routing of direct mailing campaigns to site selection for big box stores. Critically, by aggregating census data at the geographic scale of a CDP, the design of the CDP impacts the spatial distribution of all of these forms of commercial activity, governmental funding, and policy. Thus, despite the sometimes inscrutable methods behind their definition, the design of a CDP can meaningfully impact the lived realities of the population within, in a myriad of ways. Shape and content forge a complex reciprocity.

Linear Cities

Another instance in which population management and design at the geographic scale were complexly interrelated can be found in the work of members of the early twentieth century Russian architectural organization, the Association of Contemporary Architects (OSA). With noteworthy leaders such as Moisei Ginzburg, Aleksei Gan, and the Vesnin brothers, OSA is most often remembered for championing Russian Constructivism, a materialist movement closely allied to socialist and Marxist principles. In its early years, questions about how to design collective housing in order to eradicate class differences and gender inequality often dominated the OSA discourse. This early focus shifted in 1928, when Joseph Stalin launched the first Five Year Plan for Soviet economic development.[20] Stalin's plan sought to radically expand industrialization, engaging more and more of the population within contemporary

22. Kopp has noted that this ambition to eradicate the urban-rural divide was indebted to the ideas of Friedrich Engels, and his goals for socialist society. Kopp, 172-173. See also Hudson, 63-65.

23. Hudson, 63-65.

24. Okhitovich was influenced by the Spanish architect and urban planner Arturo Soria y Mata (1844-1920), who first conceived of the idea of linear cities running along infrastructural lines in 1882.

25. Kopp explained that Leonidov's Magnitogorsk was not a precise application of the tenets of either the "urbanist" or "deurbanist" schools of thought, but something of a combination between the two. Nevertheless, the circulation of Leonidov's highly compelling drawings, and the strict linear organization of the city design he proposed, has made his Magnitogorsk proposal the most emblematic of the Russian linear city proposals. Kopp, 197-198.

26. Hudson, 65.

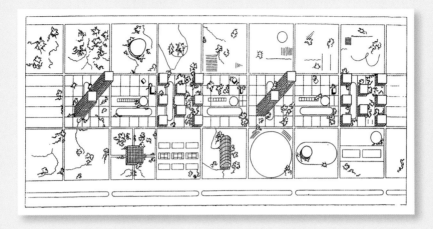

Ivan Leonidov, Linear City Magnitogorsk Proposal, 1930

modes of production. Understanding the amount of large-scale development such an expansion would entail, urbanization quickly emerged as a pressing concern among some OSA members.[21] The division between dense, urban, industrialized cities and diffuse, rural, pre-industrial villages that characterized Russia's vast territorial expanse rose to dominate the OSA discussion. For some OSA members, such a division was doubly problematic. The division unevenly enrolled the population within industrialized modes of production, and since the Marxist principles to which OSA members adhered understood modes of production to be formative of political ideology, the divide between rural and urban territories prohibited the population from consolidating as a single, collective public of the communist state.[22] Residents of cities were engaged in industry, but were often living in dense, unsanitary and inhumane conditions. Meanwhile, residents of more rural territories had access to nature and open space, but were engaged in retrograde modes of production and their attendant social organizations that often reinforced inequality along lines of class and sex. Urbanization was the appropriate technology to unite this urban-rural divide.[23]

The OSA architect and theorist Mikhail Aleksandrovich Okhitovich was among the most prominent voices in the discussion about eradicating the Soviet urban-rural division. Principal theorist of a division of OSA architects who have been labeled the "deurbanists," Okhitovich championed the design of "Ribbon Settlements" that would run parallel to new infrastructural lines across the nation from existing urban centers deep into the surrounding countryside.[24] As elaborated through designs by OSA members Moisei Ginzburg, Mikhail Barshch, and most famously in an evolved form by Ivan Leonidov in his design for Magnitogorsk,[25] Ribbon Settlements often entailed repeating planning units running along infrastructural lines composing housing, production, institutions, nature, and collective space. Existing urban centers would be evacuated. They would no longer constitute dense and overcrowded concentrations of industrial production. Meanwhile, the rural village would also be no more, eliminating the milieu of pre-industrial society valuable only to contemporary modes of production as a site of resource extraction. As historian Hugh D. Hudson, Jr. has noted: "The eventual results would be a cityless, nation of contiguous communities distributed alongside unspoiled natural surroundings."[26] Urban and rural populations would be merged as a single public of the socialist state, eradicating ideological difference and inequality by gender and class, all through the instrumental design of patterns of urbanization. Shape and content forge a complex reciprocity.

Shaped Places
A dialogue between shape and content, urban and rural territories, population and the figuration of geographic precinct, runs throughout the otherwise unrelated episodes from history and current events above. While drawn from differing times, disciplines, and contexts, these themes profoundly resonate with the spatial politics of the present. In contemporary American society, political geography is increasingly divided along urban and rural lines, often by policy and by design. This geographic schism reiterates and amplifies sharply divided ideology, fracturing the body politic into a dysfunctional segmentation of disparate populations, publics and counter publics, each with their own entrenched opinions and beliefs. So too, the urban-rural divide often coincides with differing racial demographics, also by design. The nation's legacy of redlining and white flight has reinforced many urban areas as concentrations of populations of color, even while others are home to a largely white liberal elite, and suburban and rural areas are dominated by white conservatives. Our city streets are alive with Black Lives Matter demonstrations while suburban megachurches swell; MAGA hats dot our pastures while highrises reverberate with the hum of NPR.

In the urban design provocations that follow, lessons from the above episodes are borrowed, interwoven, and applied. Extending the OSA commitment to Ribbon Settlements as a technology to unite a divided population, the designs assert the possibility that urbanization might place ideological division into political dialogue. The proposals are both facetious and earnest. While not intended to be realized, they are meant to provoke awareness of how the spatial fabrics of Americans' daily lives enforce their political ideologies and have been used to divide and marginalize vulnerable segments of society. What follows speculates on how these spatialities might be renegotiated at an urban scale.

Shaped Places of Carroll County New Hampshire has three sites, each a Census Place in New Hampshire—Sanbornville, Union, and Conway. In each site, formal strategies from one of Frank Stella's Irregular Polygon canvases have been applied to the shape of the eponymous Census Place. The results are zoning maps in which differently colored bands indicate geographically scaled swaths of territory, 200 feet in depth, of differing urban programs such as housing, production, agriculture, civic institutions, and consumerism. These zoning maps have been represented in the form of three identically scaled paintings. Each zoning map is accompanied by a ribbon city planning module that has been designed to elide rural and urban populations in unique ways. Color-coded to correspond to the zoning maps, the modules are intended to be deployed along the bands in the maps, intricately contorting to the shape of their geographic host. Within each resulting city, frequently divergent lifestyles and patterns of development would be combined, collided, and forced into coexistence. Inhabitants would find themselves perpetually confronted with difference, under the suspicion that the urban milieu might prove a productive medium to reconstruct a functional body politic, by design. Shape and content forge a complex reciprocity.

JEM
COIN LAUNDRY
TENTSMITHS
Maggio Hair Studio
The Child Advocacy Center
Of Carroll County
"protecting children, promoting justice"

CONWAY FIRE

BID N
HARRIS
JoeBiden.com

Shaped Places

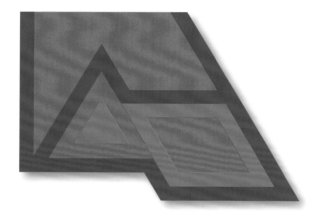

Sanbornville
Frank Stella
1966

Sanbornville, NH
Incorporated
1774

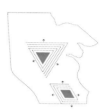

Offset

Offset

Continuity of color

Continuity of color

Sanbornville, Sanbornville
EXTENTS
2020

Sanbornville, Sanbornville
EXTENTS
2020

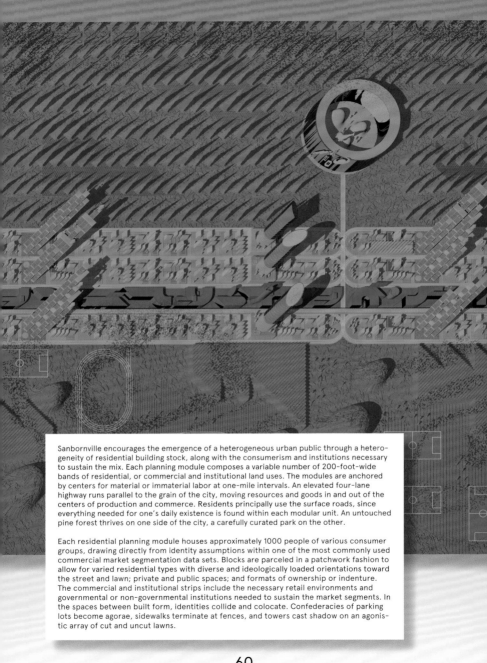

Sanbornville encourages the emergence of a heterogeneous urban public through a hetero-geneity of residential building stock, along with the consumerism and institutions necessary to sustain the mix. Each planning module composes a variable number of 200-foot-wide bands of residential, or commercial and institutional land uses. The modules are anchored by centers for material or immaterial labor at one-mile intervals. An elevated four-lane highway runs parallel to the grain of the city, moving resources and goods in and out of the centers of production and commerce. Residents principally use the surface roads, since everything needed for one's daily existence is found within each modular unit. An untouched pine forest thrives on one side of the city, a carefully curated park on the other.

Each residential planning module houses approximately 1000 people of various consumer groups, drawing directly from identity assumptions within one of the most commonly used commercial market segmentation data sets. Blocks are parceled in a patchwork fashion to allow for varied residential types with diverse and ideologically loaded orientations toward the street and lawn; private and public spaces; and formats of ownership or indenture. The commercial and institutional strips include the necessary retail environments and governmental or non-governmental institutions needed to sustain the market segments. In the spaces between built form, identities collide and colocate. Confederacies of parking lots become agorae, sidewalks terminate at fences, and towers cast shadow on an agonis-tic array of cut and uncut lawns.

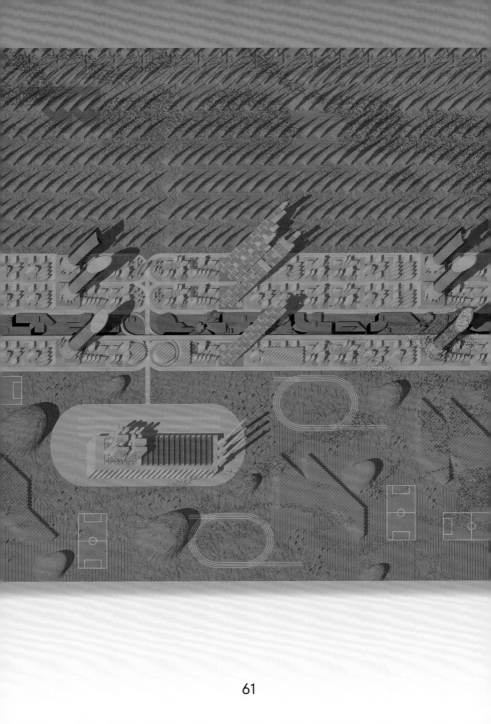

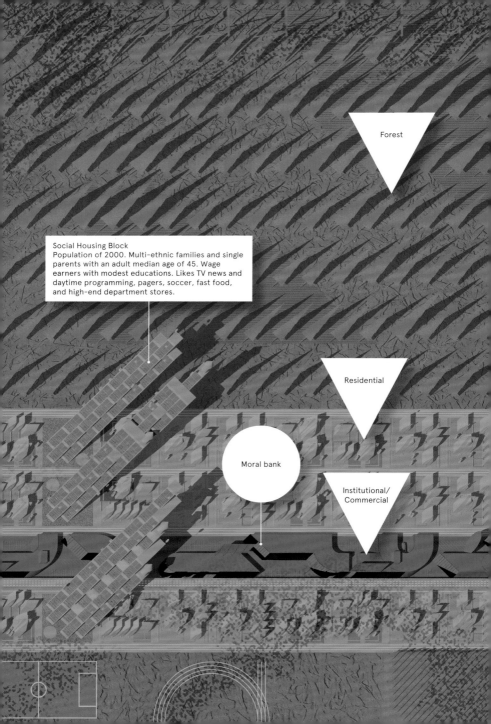

Forest

Social Housing Block
Population of 2000. Multi-ethnic families and single parents with an adult median age of 45. Wage earners with modest educations. Likes TV news and daytime programming, pagers, soccer, fast food, and high-end department stores.

Residential

Moral bank

Institutional/
Commercial

Mid-rise Office
Immaterial production.1.5 million gross square feet of Class A office space, suitable for insurance companies, advertising agencies, hedge fund management, and entertainment law firms.

House-in-Town
Household population of 2. Childless middle-aged couples with lucrative blue-collar jobs and modestly priced houses. Likes to fish and hunt in the day and stay home to watch TV at night. Buys boats, campers, motorcycles, and pickup trucks.

re

Cronuts

ATMs, more ATMs

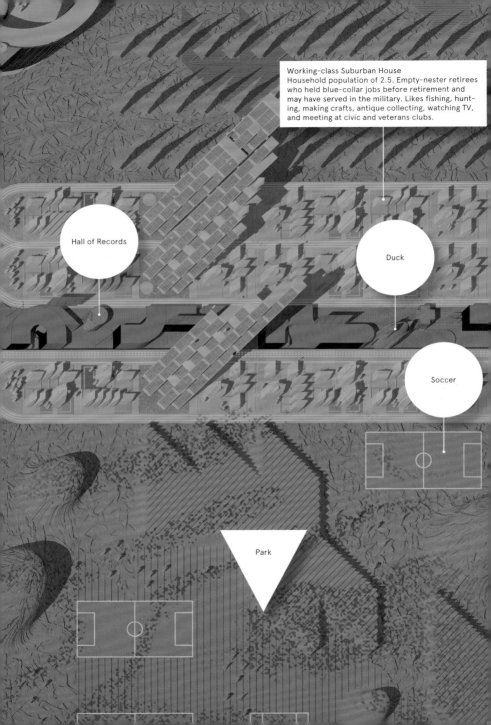

Working-class Suburban House
Household population of 2.5. Empty-nester retirees who held blue-collar jobs before retirement and may have served in the military. Likes fishing, hunting, making crafts, antique collecting, watching TV, and meeting at civic and veterans clubs.

Hall of Records

Duck

Soccer

Park

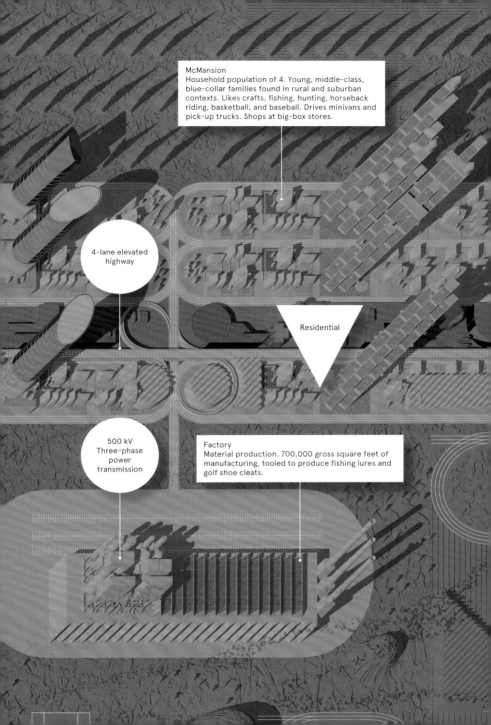

McMansion
Household population of 4. Young, middle-class, blue-collar families found in rural and suburban contexts. Likes crafts, fishing, hunting, horseback riding, basketball, and baseball. Drives minivans and pick-up trucks. Shops at big-box stores.

4-lane elevated highway

Residential

500 kV Three-phase power transmission

Factory
Material production. 700,000 gross square feet of manufacturing, tooled to produce fishing lures and golf shoe cleats.

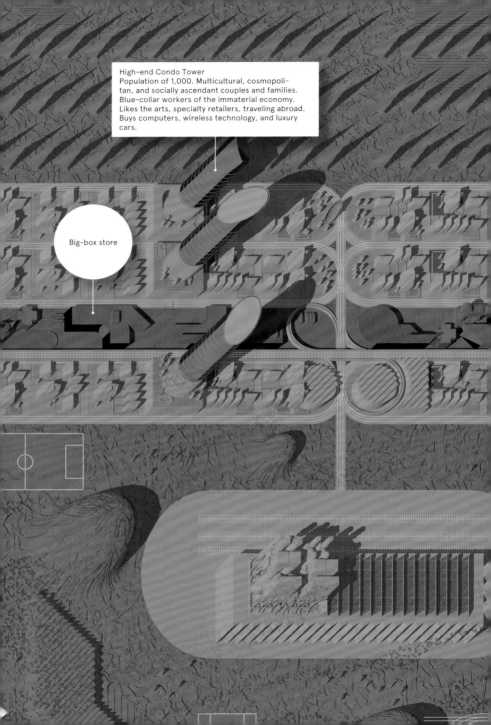

High-end Condo Tower
Population of 1,000. Multicultural, cosmopolitan, and socially ascendant couples and families. Blue-collar workers of the immaterial economy. Likes the arts, specialty retailers, traveling abroad. Buys computers, wireless technology, and luxury cars.

Big-box store

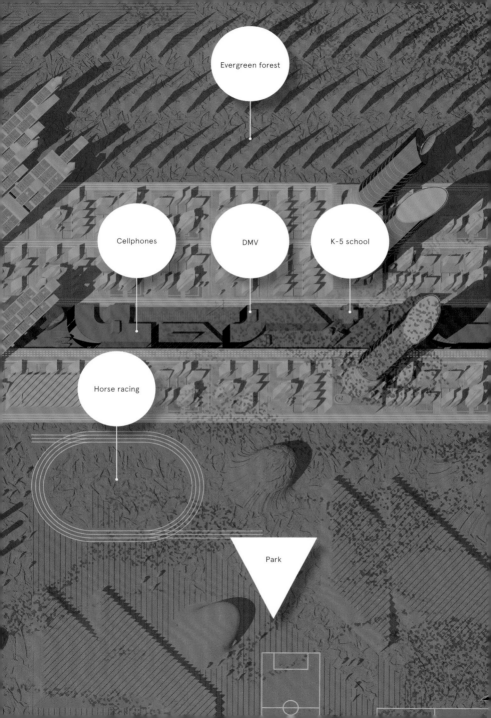

Evergreen forest

Cellphones

DMV

K-5 school

Horse racing

Park

Sending a Sunday email to Madison (away in her third semester at Vassar), while planning the holidays in Bermuda. Glassy towers rise in the background (reflecting one's own), while in the middle-distance: picket fences, vinyl siding, a sea of asphalt, taquerias, golf clubs, boots, whizzing traffic, and above-ground pools (there should be a law). Closeouts everywhere. Sous vide bubbles inaudibly in the kitchen.

The smell of diesel and Roundup. What's left of a late summer fishing trip, nightcrawlers in crunched cans of Highlife still in the hull. La Reina del Sur glowing through some windows. Lawn edgers, Harleys, somebody's Quinceañera. Open garages are man caves with beer fridges and TVs. Skateboards everywhere and sidewalks interrupted by lawns full of weeds.

Fishing bob blocking the front door of the DMV. ATMs, pawnshops, cash for gold. Wigs and plus. Golf cleats, Club América, Le Creuset. Pickups, SUVs, sensible sedans, matchbox Ferrari. Triple height entries with dramatic chandeliers, and grills in the front or back yards. A hard day's work ending at the stripmall bar. A competitive advantage from The Princeton Review.

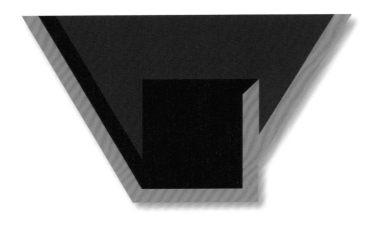

Union
Frank Stella
1966

Union, NH
Incorporated
1774

Literal Shape

Depicted Shape

Offset

Offset

Continuity of color

Continuity of color

Union, Union
EXTENTS
2020

Shaped Places

Union, Union
EXTENTS
2020

Union is a city of Ha-ha Houses: city in the front, town and country in the back. Each 200-foot-wide planning module composes twenty-seven residential structures with a population of 100 people, negotiating a sectional sleight-of-hand in order to appear as urban towers on one side, and semi-urban or suburban unattached houses on the other. Such formal acrobatics allow the buildings to host a diversity of lifestyles, drawing directly from identity assumptions within one of the most commonly used commercial market segmentation data sets. Midblock voids carved into the buildings serve, alternately, as suburban backyards or urban rooftop gardens. In these spaces, identities and their associated accoutrements intersperse, while the voids align to form viewing corridors down the length of the module. These views afford a theatre of difference-in-action.

Two large figural structures interrupt the continuity of Ha-ha Houses in each one mile-long planning module. These buildings contain stacked big-box stores, ground level boutique retail, parking garages, offices, and various governmental and non-governmental institutions—all of the lifestyle infrastructure necessary to sustain the identities in the Ha-ha Houses. On one side of the city, residents find industrial agriculture, hunting, and NASCAR. Chicken. On the other side, an urban park with soccer pitches and cultural institutions. Pigeon.

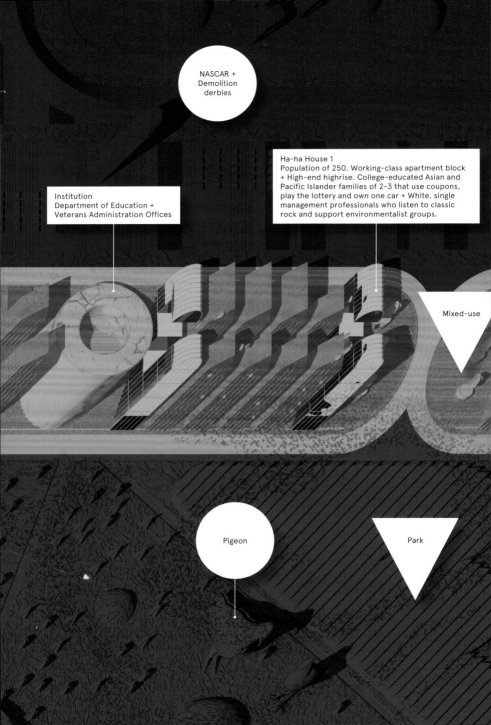

NASCAR +
Demolition
derbies

Ha-ha House 1
Population of 250. Working-class apartment block
+ High-end highrise. College-educated Asian and
Pacific Islander families of 2-3 that use coupons,
play the lottery and own one car + White, single
management professionals who listen to classic
rock and support environmentalist groups.

Institution
Department of Education +
Veterans Administration Offices

Mixed-use

Pigeon

Park

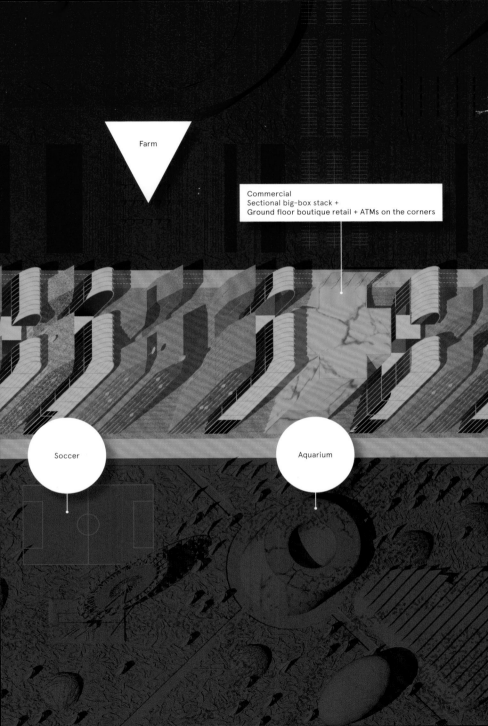

Farm

Commercial
Sectional big-box stack +
Ground floor boutique retail + ATMs on the corners

Soccer

Aquarium

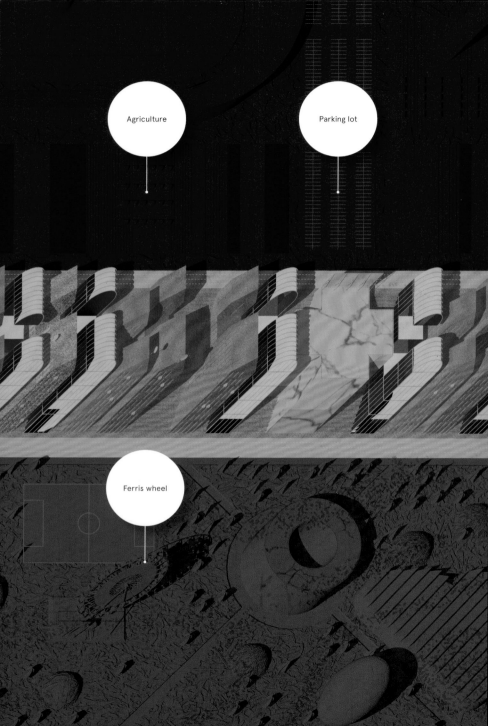

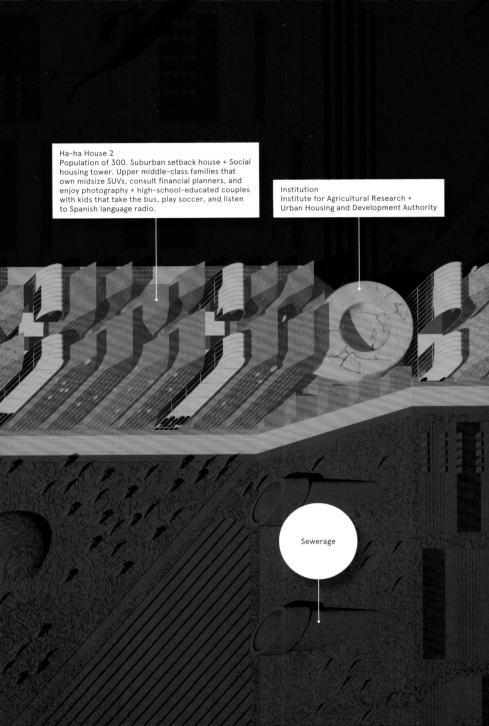

Ha-ha House 2
Population of 300. Suburban setback house + Social housing tower. Upper middle-class families that own midsize SUVs, consult financial planners, and enjoy photography + high-school-educated couples with kids that take the bus, play soccer, and listen to Spanish language radio.

Institution
Institute for Agricultural Research + Urban Housing and Development Authority

Sewerage

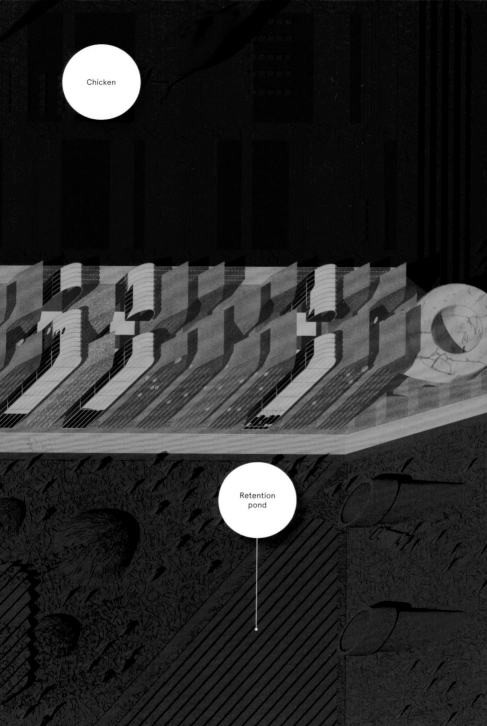

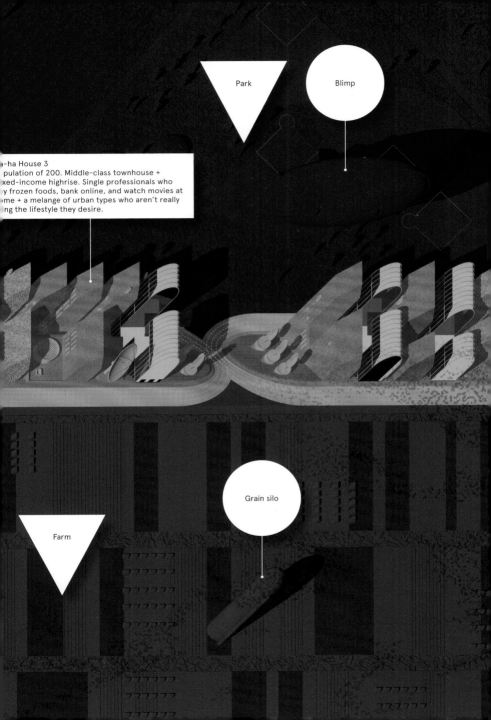

Park

Blimp

-ha House 3
pulation of 200. Middle-class townhouse +
xed-income highrise. Single professionals who
y frozen foods, bank online, and watch movies at
me + a melange of urban types who aren't really
ng the lifestyle they desire.

Grain silo

Farm

That same Ikea console. Drawers filled with generations of iPhones. The smell of hot dogs and charcoal. Strolling passersby with bluetooth, or big family camped out for the weekend with radio. Pottery Barn and Restoration Hardware visible through big glassy windows, or the backs of ill-placed bunk beds crammed into the kids' room. Trash cans overfull with styrofoam, newspapers, chicken bones, and nonfat skinny lattes.

Domino's Pizza at a shotgun wedding. F-150 altar, and flowergirl daughter from a second marriage. Honda Odysseys in the demolition derby. Join the Future Farmers of America or the Model UN. Terraces are a gradient of Monsanto content. Shakespeare in the Park, somewhere in the distance. Masons, Knights of Columbus, Elks, Oprah's Book Club. A Walmart right on top of a Target, but both losing business because Amazon.

A cow in the median strip, and lingering dust on floor-ceiling-windows from the spring tillage. Someone's curry, toy trucks, abandoned appliances, and a tractor tire as a table. Tucker Carlson, Terry Gross, or José Díaz-Balart. Errant bales of hay tumble down stairs, toppling Karen and birdwatcher. Pushing F22 to capture the sun setting over soccer fields and grain silos.

Conway
Frank Stella
1966

Conway, NH
Incorporated
1765

Literal Shape

Depicted Shape

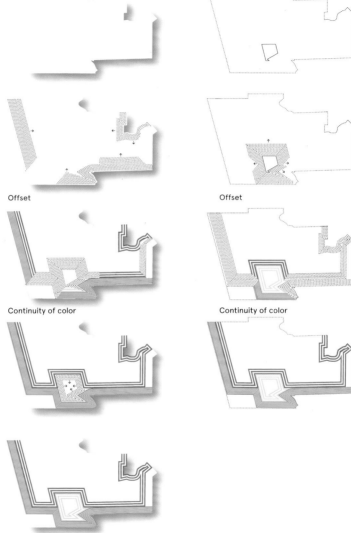

Offset

Offset

Continuity of color

Continuity of color

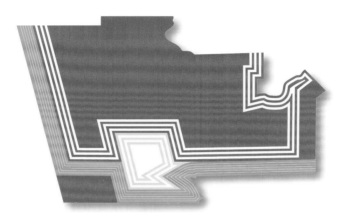

Conway, Conway
EXTENTS
2020

Conway, Conway
EXTENTS
2020

Conway is a city for machinic vision. The proposal is composed of 200-foot-wide bands, each zoned for a unique hybrid of habitation and horticulture. Here, the linear urban pattern has been converted to individuated cellular land parcels. Each cell hosts a nature-culture that mixes urbane and bucolic, providing environments for specific identities drawn from one of the most commonly used commercial market segmentation data sets. In this pixelated urban assemblage, people become data-points. Towers housing diverse market segments drip with agriculture–from commercial farming to more kale for the smoothie. Nobody knows how many people live in this city as identities collide in a culture of congestion. Highways twist and contort to the city's cellular logic above gardens, wilderness preserves, and crops below. Hovering drones capture data-images that are isomorphic to the city's systems of organization.

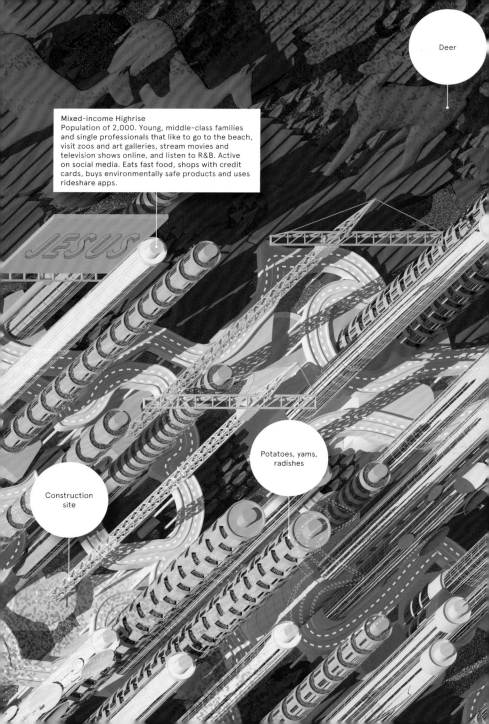

Deer

Mixed-income Highrise
Population of 2,000. Young, middle-class families and single professionals that like to go to the beach, visit zoos and art galleries, stream movies and television shows online, and listen to R&B. Active on social media. Eats fast food, shops with credit cards, buys environmentally safe products and uses rideshare apps.

JESUS

Potatoes, yams, radishes

Construction site

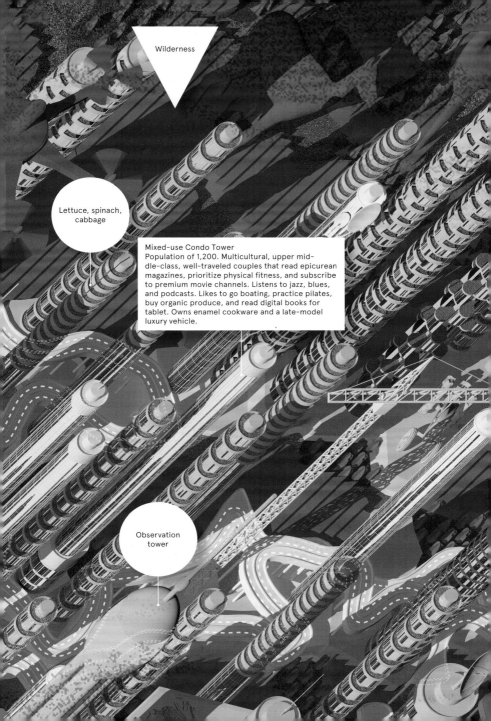

Wilderness

Lettuce, spinach, cabbage

Mixed-use Condo Tower
Population of 1,200. Multicultural, upper middle-class, well-traveled couples that read epicurean magazines, prioritize physical fitness, and subscribe to premium movie channels. Listens to jazz, blues, and podcasts. Likes to go boating, practice pilates, buy organic produce, and read digital books for tablet. Owns enamel cookware and a late-model luxury vehicle.

Observation tower

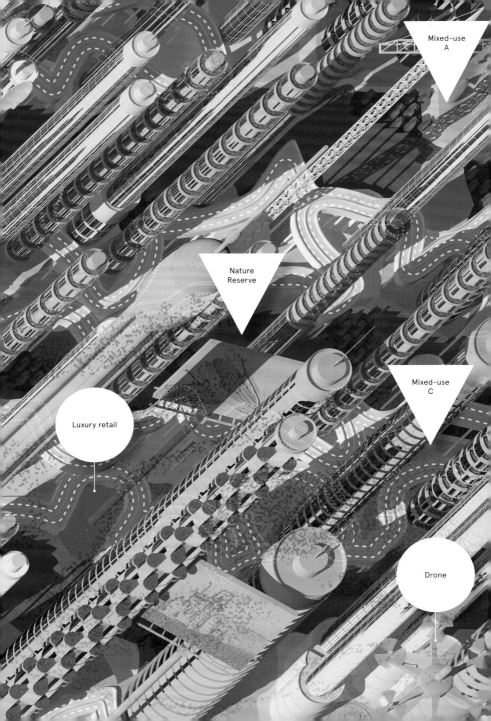

Mixed-use
A

Nature
Reserve

Mixed-use
C

Luxury retail

Drone

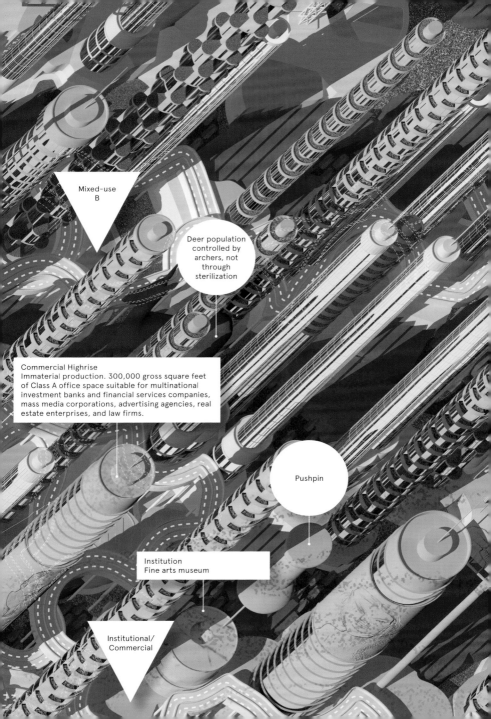

Mixed-use
B

Deer population controlled by archers, not through sterilization

Commercial Highrise
Immaterial production. 300,000 gross square feet of Class A office space suitable for multinational investment banks and financial services companies, mass media corporations, advertising agencies, real estate enterprises, and law firms.

Pushpin

Institution
Fine arts museum

Institutional/
Commercial

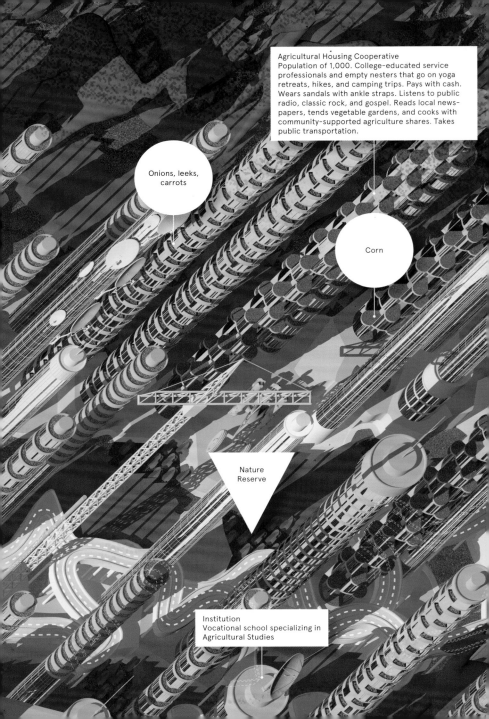

Agricultural Housing Cooperative
Population of 1,000. College-educated service professionals and empty nesters that go on yoga retreats, hikes, and camping trips. Pays with cash. Wears sandals with ankle straps. Listens to public radio, classic rock, and gospel. Reads local news-papers, tends vegetable gardens, and cooks with community-supported agriculture shares. Takes public transportation.

Onions, leeks, carrots

Corn

Nature Reserve

Institution
Vocational school specializing in Agricultural Studies

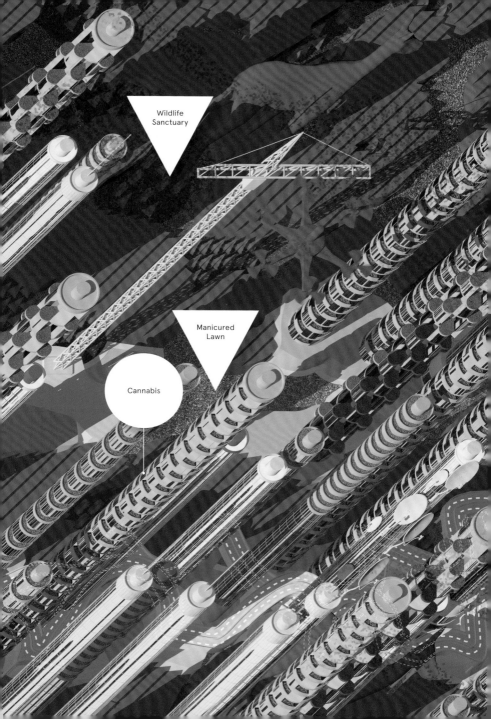

Wildlife
Sanctuary

Manicured
Lawn

Cannabis

Leaving at 9am to avoid rush hour during the harvest. Sprinklers loaded with nitrogen fertilizer. Canning corn before catching the Stella retrospective. Stop at Cabela's on the 25th floor. Miles Davis and a white bean casserole with a glass of wine on the weekend. In the spring, purple martins cross flight paths with pigeons and drones.

Yoga on the balcony under grow lights. Eggplants, microgreens, bean shoots, bok choy. Avocado toast in fellowship hall after a long sermon. Setting up the kid's old room with a treadmill and a table for scrapbooking. Taxidermy trophies from last year's kill fill the lobby.

American drivers hit 1.9 million deer on the road every year. There are 150,000 words in the Spanish language. Per capita, Americans consume approximately 1.5 pounds of spinach each year. At 200 bushels per acre, every acre of corn absorbs 8 tons of carbon dioxide.

Conway
Marketplace

Chicken and Egg

Clare Lyster

Chicken

The choice of a line as the organizational system for the three cities that comprise Shaped Places of Carroll County says much about EXTENTS's approach to urbanism. At its core, the linear city is an infrastructural proposition, in that repetition, territorial structuring, communication flows, and metabolic processes take precedent in how the built environment is configured, rather than the articulation and aggregation of form. While a line can create an identifiable figure, and many linear cities offer visionary configurations, line is less of an ideological choice (line for the sake of line) than the fallout of other pressing agendas. The hypothesis is that configuring the city is less a representational and autonomous act than one rooted in wider geo-spatial and socio-economic processes. In other words, shape follows content. Many historic examples, like those mentioned in this publication, re-scripted the city through the reorganization of industrial production by advocating new labor and material flows, promoting rural densification to alleviate overcrowding in major metropolitan areas, or pursuing a balanced and healthy lifestyle with an emphasis on the integration of agriculture. Since most emphasized the role of mobility networks, information, communication, and transportation conduits were often deployed as primary structuring agents for design. By envisioning how one would live alongside a highway or over a train line, linearapoli emphasized horizontal continuity in terms of territorial footprint. Some stretched infinitely outwards from municipal regions. Edgar Chambless's *Roadtown* from 1909 stretched from New York to Philadelphia; Peter Eisenman and Michael Graves's speculative project from 1965 spread for 22 miles across New Jersey; Höweler and Yoon's *Shareway 2030* from 2012 ran for 450 miles linking Boston and Washington, D.C. As a result, the linear city is often positioned as a geographical construct rather than an architectural entity. Infrastructural flow is its primary integer.

Infrastructural urbanism has had many fathers since Arturo Soria Y Mata's linear city prototype from 1884, but three periods in the 20th century stand out. The Metabolist movement from the late 1950s to the early 1970s in Japan popularized the megastructure as a viable urban formation for post-war rebuilding. In Metabolist

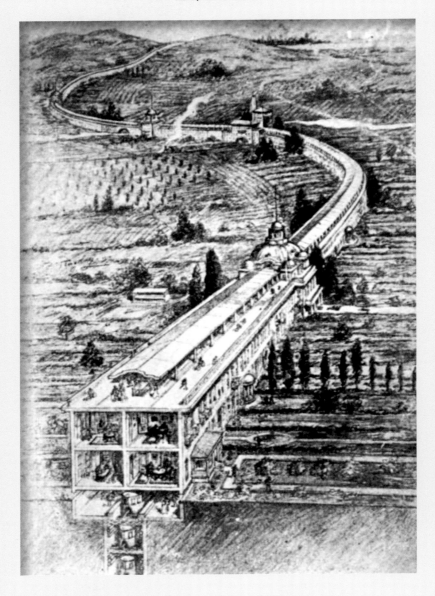

Roadtown, Perspective Drawing, 1909. Edgar Chambless. Source: Public Domain.

projects, massive structural support systems were conceived as scaffolds into which smaller scaled living units were located. These support systems, which took many forms (vertical core, sprawling grid, horizontal spine) were infrastructural because they were massive in scale, heavy (usually made from concrete), and fixed, like a sort of artificial geology. Meanwhile, the modular living units (the architecture) were lighter so that they could be swapped out, recycled, or changed over time.

The radical projects of the mid 1960s and early 1970s by Archigram and Archizoom looked at emerging technological infrastructure and early computation systems as agents for new forms of distributed urbanism. These projects deployed softer networks (electronics, cables, fax machines, computers) to envision smart environments (surfaces and grids) for nomadic lifestyles. There, infrastructure was so pervasive and critical to urban life that architecture was dematerialized, if not eliminated altogether. Unlike the Metabolists, infrastructure was no longer a support for urban living or in service to architecture. Rather, infrastructure was equal to, if not superseding, architecture as the primary building block of the built environment.

More recently, in the late 1990s and early aughts, infrastructure was again repurposed for a new generation. Stan Allen's essay "Infrastructural Urbanism" formulated a sensibility to city-making, moving away from known architectural tropes and representational techniques to deploy strategies more readily associated with the design and implementation of infrastructural space. According to Allen, this way of thinking about the built environment would promote a more material engagement with the city. Interestingly enough, these included many of the same principles espoused by linear city planning: the repetition of units, the agency of surface, fluidity, and indeterminacy. Concomitantly, forays by other architects and landscape architects augmented this way of thinking by emphasizing the material manifestation of natural and networked flows (James Corner's essay, "Terra Fluxus" stands out here); landscape as a vehicle for planning (Charles Waldheim); the incorporation of metabolic processes (Erik Swyngedouw); and ground as a support for urban form (@scape by Rem Koolhaas and

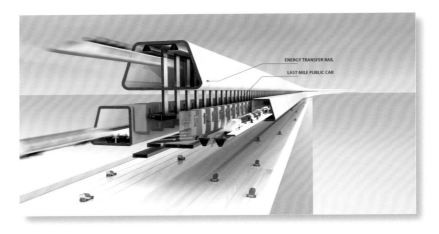

Höweler + Yoon, BosWash: Shareway 2030, Section Perspective, 2012
A proposed bundled conduit stretching along I-90 between Boston and Washington, DC with share-based structures that offer flexible and efficient housing, work and social spaces. The spine is a multi-layered and multi-scaled conduit composing highspeed freight and passenger flows, as well as the all-important "last mile" delivery options. Major nodes in support of the spine occupy leftover spaces formed by the turning radii of the high-speed train.

Alex Wall's theorization of the urban surface are key contributions here). Common to these was the notion that the city demanded a different sort of design intelligence outside of architecture that could better handle late capitalist transformations—from global flows of capital to international production—combined with the increasing demand for green systems and the need for more flexible planning at the neighborhood scale in the aftermath of the failure of many modern housing projects. As such, infrastructural (and landscape) urbanism emphasized loops, flows, frameworks, and constructed surfaces as organizational devices—using representational methods that described the city through dynamic time-space formats and processes of flow rather than figure-ground techniques. During a period when architecture's internal discourse focused on form, the infrastructural approach became an alternative mode for designers who preferred to explore the city through the indexical rather than composition and geometry. That practice

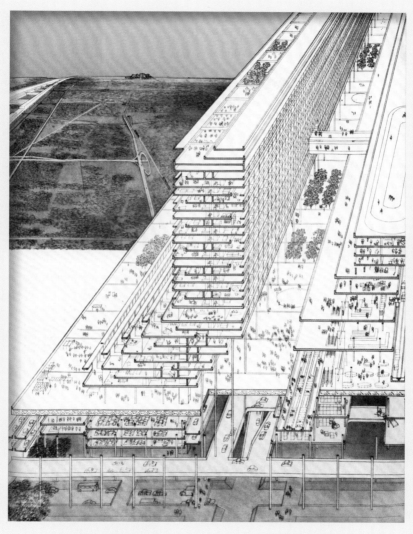

Jersey Corridor, Section Perspective, 1964-1968. Michael Graves and Peter D. Eisenman.
A 21-mile monolithic city composing two parallel bars (the lower one for industry and the higher one for living and shopping) that linked New Brunswick to Trenton, New Jersey. The project was conceived as a prototype for a new kind of city that could manage sprawl in the northeast corridor. While utopian and megastructural in scale, the project was designed around human activity, such as a 15-minute walking distance. The project was also ahead of its time in terms of parking and freight handling facilities that were located in the lower platform, freeing up the upper levels for open space and community interaction.

could be expanded to incorporate a wider set of inputs and outputs motivated a younger generation of architects to reclaim systems thinking as a vehicle for city-making. In concert, an entire new catalog of spatial tropes—loops, fields, bands, patterns, patches, mats, grids, matrices, and lines—(re)emerged, eschewing composition for openness and advocating formats as opposed to forms. Shape, while not absent, took a back seat as meaning was not driven by formal gesture, in and of itself, but by operational strategy.

In the context of this short genealogy, I would like to interrogate some of the ways that the three Carroll County projects by EXTENTS embrace an infrastructural sensibility, or not, as the case may be.

Like some sort of mysterious marker, *Sanbornville* is an abstraction in the landscape—a precisely calibrated straight line that bleeds across the host canvas with unrelenting fervor. Like an electrical cable of hot, neutral, and ground wires, its three sub-bands of color never mix, each as rational and machined as the next. In plan, *Sanbornville* is the most absolute manifestation of a linear configuration, and as a result the most honest and pure of the trilogy. No contamination between the strands, as programs (houses, office, and landscape) politely adhere to their boundaries. Zoning is managed with razor sharp edges amplified by transportation infrastructure. There is no ambiguity about the genealogy of this stroke, as we are immediately reminded of the crazy and fantastic ambition of the six-mile grid in Jefferson's imperial lattice—a continentally scaled mega-field borne out of the 1785 Public Land Survey System that was to organize half of the continental United States. According to geographer Denis Cosgrove, and not unlike the linear city, the Jeffersonian grid "only makes sense from the air."[1] *Sanbornville* is the infrastructural city in its most expanded and diagrammatic form—a universal and engineered right of way that, like a highway or railroad, is measured and scaled to handle the endlessness of the American landscape.

An infrastructural approach to city-making yields hybrid spaces—new typologies of space that don't fall neatly into a disciplinary category but instead are formed by the integration of different spatial and scalar tropes. In the case of the linear city, one might ask if it is geography, landscape, infrastructure or architecture. In truth, it's a compilation of all four, a combinatory space that affords a reading of the city that, according to Swiss architect Marc Angelil, allows fragments to merge into a singular entity.[2] In this context, the ha-ha house in *Union*, the second of the three proposals for Carroll County, stands out. The ha-ha is an agricultural infrastructure used to separate two landscape areas, typically one used for pleasure and one used for animal grazing. Best described as a ditch with a retaining wall on one side, the ha-ha separates a slope into two discontinuous levels, yet preserves visual continuity across the extended terrain. In being simultaneously an infrastructural edge and a landscape, the ha-ha is an exemplary hybrid that doubles as a disguise. Through what Clutter and Peñarroyo call a sectional sleight-of-hand, it's an optical illusion to conceal difference. Likewise in *Union*, the ha-ha house (version 2) is cast as a typological trick to conceal a duality. One side reveals a suburban-scale domain of two floors, the other a multi-story high-rise. In this moment the ha-ha is realized as a spatial trick that allows the two conditions and their respective subjects (urbanite and suburbanite) to symbiotically co-exist. In this way, it successfully manifests the political motive that underlies the project—to merge living conditions and contexts (red and blue) that typically sit in opposition to each other.

The third project, *Conway*, reflects an infrastructural approach by interpreting the solid band of the line less as a continuous stripe and more as a pixelated matrix. Here the pixels behave as a non-compositional assemblage, like a field of points or a swarm of colored nodes that are seemingly chaotically clustered. Although extruded as tall cylinders, their varying heights, repetition, and close proximity resist being read as singularities. Instead, they

1. Denis Cosgrove, "The Measures of America" in James Corner and Alex S. MacLean, eds,. *Taking Measures Across the American Landscape* (New York: Yale University Press, 1996), 3-14.
2. Marc Angelil, "Hybrid Morphologies: Infrastructure, Architecture, Landscape" in *Daidlos* 73, 1999, 16-25.
3. R. E. Somol, "All Systems GO!: The Terminal Nature of Contemporary Urbanism," in Julia Czerniak, ed., *Downsview Park Toronto* (Munich: Prestel Verlag, 2001), 126-135.
4. Michael Fried, "Shape as Form," in *Artforum*, November 1966, pp. 18-27.

appear as a pixelated constellation of undulating rods that, despite being color-coded for specific use, could in fact host interchangeable program—vertical agriculture, housing, office space, data storage, or combinations thereof. I'm reminded of OMA and Bruce Mau's *Tree City*, a winning project for the Downsview Park competition in 2000, where varying densities of dots are deployed across the site as a syntax for future events to happen. Akin to a code rather than container, the pattern implies rather than dictates; suggests rather than prescribes. In being less deliberate about form, *Conway* embodies the key words of infrastructural thinking from the late 1990s (Allen and Corner et al): emergent systems, with an organization that is more framework than masterplan, more field than figure, and more forest than building. Not only that, but it doubles-down on its infrastructural lineage, in that the 3d printers and cranes, perhaps programmed by AI to fabricate the city, evoke memories of Archigram's fetishization of industrial infrastructure as an agent for a future posthuman city. This means that shape is now smart and driven by a script, while meaning is decided by a machine. A knot of roadways weaves in and around the base, implying communication and relationships across a larger territory.

Egg

In time, the lauded credits of the infrastructural approach were reassessed and projected as weaknesses, with some claiming that the agency of process, flow, performance, and time was overdetermined. It was simply naïve to think that a city could design itself. Infrastructural strategies left too much up to externalities and contingency and not enough to design. Too much content and not enough shape.

While broadly adopting an infrastructural sensibility, yet at the same time cleverly deploying other techniques in concert, it could be said that EXTENTS confronts some of the criticisms made of the systems approach to city-making—namely that without a more promiscuous formal agenda, urbanism couldn't be advanced as a medium for design. It's no coincidence that Clutter and Peñarroyo both came of age in the early years of Robert E. Somol's tenure at the University of Illinois at Chicago (Clutter as junior faculty and

Logistical Activities Zone, Competition. Barcelona, 1996. Stan Allen.
A flexible master plan for the port terminal in Barcelona presented as a user's manual for the future development of the site. Six strategies are proposed. Four of these explore how the site is formatted as an infrastructural space: Surface (patches, matrix, mosaic, and extent), Organization (edges, corridors, and network), Structure (Roof and Frame), and Repetition (fields and variation); while two strategies deal with program and use from the perspective of Service and Anticipation.

Instead of figure/ ground drawings of fixed spaces and boundaries, emphasis was placed on the overlay of scripts and notational representation anticipating multiple possible scenarios for the site over time that, according to Allen, would enable a "loose fit" of organization and program.

The image selected here shows the superimposition of the strategies that combine to articulate the site as a "structured field," with sufficient specificity to imply use, yet flexible enough to offer multiple possibilities.

Image courtesy of Stan Allen Architect.

Gerco de Ruijter: Grid Corrections
A series of aerial images capture the corrections required to resolve the Jeffersonian Grid with the curvature of the earth's surface. The corrections that occur at 20-mile intervals illustrate the interdependency of
a system (grid) with form (earth as canvas). Source: Gerco de Ruijter, *Grid Corrections*, Rotterdam: NAI010
Publishers, 2019

Peñarroyo as a student) at a time when Somol, in a review of the aforementioned Downsview Park Competition, expressed the neutrality of the indexical project by the phrase, "look ma, no hands."[3] It is in this oscillation between staging and shaping or field and figure that the Shaped Places of Carroll Country might be best debated.

Shape appears in arched facades, sawtooth roofs and stepped-scapes, while embossed landscapes are presented as figurative geoglyphs akin to alien crop circles. Landmarks and icons appear in the form of oversized animals and foul, as well as grain silos and other industrial artifacts. Semantic gestures in the form of blown-up cultural symbols (a giant skateboard) sit side-by-side with scattered bricolage from cars to agricultural elements. Here, infrastructure plays back stage to the articulation of objecthood.

In addition, on careful analysis of the zoning maps, which were created through reference to the original paintings by Frank Stella, one realizes the linear bands don't extend that far. The 200-foot-wide strips double back in response to their host geography, like the Jefferson Grid forced into distortion by the earth's curvature. In *Sanbornville* and *Union*, the bands contort and shift to produce corners, vertices and figural voids, while in *Conway* they hug an edge to yield a large interior. Unlike other versions of the linear city, where territorial nuances are ignored by the abstraction of the line, here geography is an active participant: it too is shaped.

The selection of drawings also tells a story. An infrastructural sensibility would inspire mobility, performance, phasing diagrams, and/or drawings that index dynamic processes and forces on the site. Instead, process is eschewed in favor of the all-encompassing bird's eye view that focuses more on the scenography and spatial politics of the different scenarios than "how" the project might work. Best described as part montage, part drawing, buildings are typologically explicit with highly articulated facades, while the curated juxtaposition of the objects on the ground exemplify how the constructed cultures of the project (red and blue) might play out: NASCAR next to food production, Trojan Horse adjacent to bird house, and a Ferrari next to a pick-up truck. The representation is cinematic, as these objects are positioned like props in a set to amplify the political desires of the project, although the lack of entourage makes it unclear what actual collectives might be initiated by the chosen binaries. It is at this level of detail—the close-ups—where the aspirations of the project are best illustrated, to the point that the regional ambition of the linear formation seems less emphatic than the fragmented juxtapositions of the micro-scenes and their narratives.

Chicken and Egg

In an era when digital, ecological, and material flows as well as transportation infrastructure dominate how we live, an infrastructural approach to city-making seems critical now more than ever. Moreover, at a time of increasing challenges, from climate change to socio-political unrest, one questions how an autonomous practice might responsibly engage with the crises in our midst. In the same way that earlier linear city projects took on important issues, contemporary urbanism must confront the complex conditions that society faces today by employing design not only to index but more significantly to speculate on some of the geo-spatial transformations (in EXTENTS's case, political differences) that are taking place around us. The word "speculate" is important here. Design can go beyond indexing and problem solving to project outcomes for contemporary issues only in tandem with shape-making techniques, including the utilization of abstract art as seen in the three proposals for Carroll County in this book. In this way, an infrastructural sensibility to the built environment is enhanced (call it infrastructure plus) toward the design of new urban configurations and collectives.

The dilemma of shape and content, or better cast here as the oscillation between object and system, is an ongoing debate on how urbanism is viewed as a critical medium. It's not that form and operation (shape and content) should be pitted against each other, but instead play off each other. Shaped Places of Carroll County puts forward an idea that urbanism can be both issue-based (content-driven) and formally authored (shaped), and that these two approaches are interdependent. Just as Michael Fried pondered whether Frank Stella's geometric lines in the Irregular Polygons paintings (1966) shaped the canvas, or if the canvas gave form to the lines. Fried surmised, "But neither kind of shape enjoys precedence over the other...both types of shape succeed or fail on exactly the same grounds...each, one might say, is implicated in the other's failure and strengthened by the other's success."[4] Shape and content forge a complex reciprocity.

2020 Presidential Election Results

Afterword

We began working on Shaped Places in the days following the 2016 Presidential election. In a context in which the political reality of the United States seemed unimaginably changed, there was comfort in meditating on how the spatial distribution of the American electorate both explains and reinforces the nation's sharply divided political ideologies. Our design speculations were never meant to be ameliorative, but as is common in satire, they were meant to vivify very serious concerns. Working on this project throughout 2020 has provided a wealth of moments of pause. It has often seemed hard to justify the relevance of speculative urban fantasy in a time when our nation's cities filled with protests for racial justice, and when our urban centers constituted the front lines for a worsening global pandemic. We are now completing this project in the aftermath of the 2020 Presidential election. As we write this afterword in late November, the election has been won but the sitting President refuses to concede. This time there is little comfort in meditating on spatio-political geography. That the nation's rural-urban divide is isomorphic to our fractured political ideology is now more wincingly obvious than ever, with one side replacing science and facts with conspiratorial innuendo that threatens to shake the foundations of our democracy. In light of all of this context, we recognize that this book might land like a bad joke. But we hope that humor will be a vehicle for sober reflection on the role, and perhaps agency, of the built environment in the constitution of our body politic. While the cities that comprise Shaped Places hold a circus mirror to the nation's political reality, we hope that in that reflection the viewer might recognize the potential for another America.

Acknowledgments

Shaped Places of Carroll County New Hampshire has slowly developed within EXTENTS over the past several years. Accordingly, we have many friends and collaborators to thank. Several prior students and employees helped us to develop the project, most notably Michael Amidon, Craig Zehr, Lucas Denit, Pedro Duhart Benavides, Anne Redmond, Reed Miller, and Maggie Cochrane. We are grateful to Chris Grimely and the team at the Pinkcomma Gallery for the opportunity to exhibit this project in the fall of 2018. John McMorrough provided comments on an early version of our work, and Enrique Ramirez provided detailed and thoughtful comments on the text included in this book. We are grateful to the 2020 ACSA Faculty Design Awards jury, Rania Ghosn, Courtney Crosson, and Jennifer Bonner for finding the project worthy of commendation. We also extend our thanks to Robert Fishman and Clare Lyster for their fantastic contributions to this publication. This work would not be possible without the vital academic environment provided by the University of Michigan Taubman College of Architecture and Urban Planning, and we have benefitted from the intellectual generosity of too many colleagues there to list. Shaped Places was supported by Taubman College, and the University of Michigan Office of Research.